The Role of NLP in Career Counseling and Professional Development

Development

By Rex Morton

Copyright Page

Published by Omniterra Media Inc

First Edition

Visit the author's website at www.rexmorton.com

For information regarding special discounts for bulk purchases, please contact Rex Morton @ Rex@rexmorton.com.

Disclaimer

This book is intended to provide information about the fields of Neuro-Linguistic Programming (NLP) and Cognitive Behavioural Therapy (CBT) and their potential integration. While the author has made every effort to ensure that the information was correct at the time of publication, the author does not assume and hereby disclaims any liability to any party for any loss, damage, or disruption caused by errors or omissions, whether such errors or omissions result from negligence, accident, or any other cause.

The contents of this book should not be used as a substitute for professional advice, diagnosis, or treatment. The reader should always consult with a qualified healthcare provider about any mental health concerns or conditions. Never disregard professional psychological or medical advice or delay in seeking it because of something you have read in this book.

The views expressed in this work are solely those of the author and do not necessarily reflect the views of the publisher, and the publisher hereby disclaims any responsibility for them.

The inclusion of websites, links, or references to other resources does not mean that the author or the publisher endorses the information the organization or website may provide or recommendations it might make. Furthermore, the author does not guarantee the accuracy of the information these resources provide.

The use of any information provided in this book is solely at your own risk.

Introduction

Welcome to "The Role of Neuro-Linguistic Programming in Career Counseling and Professional Development," a comprehensive guide designed to explore the intersection of these three critical areas. This book aims to provide insights into how Neuro-Linguistic Programming (NLP) can be leveraged in the field of career counseling and professional development, offering practical strategies, case studies, and future trends.

Career counseling and professional development are integral aspects of an individual's career trajectory. In an ever-evolving job market, the need for effective career counseling has never been more critical. It helps individuals understand their skills, interests, and potential, guiding them towards fulfilling career paths. Similarly, professional development plays a crucial role in equipping individuals with the necessary skills and knowledge to thrive in their chosen careers. It ensures that individuals continue to be competent in their profession and can navigate the changes and advancements in their field.

NLP, also known as neuro-linguistic programming, is a psychological strategy that entails studying the tactics employed by successful people and using them to accomplish one's own objectives. It links ideas, words, and behavioural patterns acquired via experience to certain results. In the context of career counseling and professional development, NLP can offer valuable tools and techniques to help individuals overcome challenges, improve communication, set achievable goals, and ultimately, advance in their careers.

In the following chapters, we will delve deeper into the principles of NLP, its role and application in career counseling, and how it can be utilized for professional development. We will explore specific NLP techniques, discuss the challenges and solutions in applying NLP in career counseling, and look at the future trends of NLP in this field.

Whether you are a career counselor, a human resource professional, a manager, or an individual interested in personal career growth, this book will provide you with a new perspective on career development strategies. It is designed to offer practical, actionable insights that can be applied in real-world scenarios to enhance career counseling outcomes and foster professional growth. Let's embark on this journey to explore the transformative potential of NLP in career counseling and professional development.

Chapter 1: Understanding Neuro-Linguistic Programming

Neuro-Linguistic Programming, commonly referred to as NLP, is a fascinating field that has been influencing various areas of personal and professional development for decades. To fully appreciate its role in career counseling and professional development, we must first understand what NLP is, its history, principles, techniques, and its role in personal development.

Definition and History of NLP

Neuro-Linguistic Programming (NLP) is a psychological approach that combines insights from cognitive and neurosciences, linguistics, and programming to facilitate personal and professional development. The term itself can be broken down into three components:

Neuro: Referring to the brain and neural network that processes our experiences.

Linguistic: Pertaining to the linguistic system through which our thoughts are coded, ordered, and given meaning.

Programming: The ability to organize our thoughts and actions in a manner to achieve specific goals and results.

NLP was developed in the 1970s by Richard Bandler, a mathematician, and John Grinder, a linguist. They were interested in understanding how certain individuals consistently achieved excellence in their respective fields. They studied successful therapists and communicators, modeling their thought processes, behaviors, and language patterns. The techniques they developed aimed to replicate these patterns of success, leading to the birth of NLP.

Principles and Techniques of NLP

NLP operates on a set of core principles. One of the fundamental assumptions is that the mind and body are part of the same system and influence each other. Another is that our perception of the world is subjective, based on our experiences and thought processes.

NLP techniques are practical applications of these principles. They include strategies like anchoring (associating emotional states with physical triggers), reframing (changing the way one perceives an event), and modeling (copying successful behaviors). These techniques aim to change unhelpful thought patterns, improve communication, and help individuals achieve their goals.

The Role of NLP in Personal Development

NLP plays a significant role in personal development. It offers tools and techniques to understand and change our thought processes, behaviors, and emotional responses. By doing so, it helps individuals overcome limiting beliefs, improve their interpersonal skills, increase self-confidence, and achieve personal goals. Whether it's enhancing communication, overcoming fears, or improving decision-making, NLP can be a powerful tool for personal growth and transformation.

In the next chapters, we will delve deeper into how these principles and techniques of NLP can be applied in the context of career counseling and professional development. We will explore how NLP can enhance career guidance strategies, facilitate professional growth, and contribute to successful career trajectories.

Career counseling is a critical component of an individual's professional journey. It provides guidance, helps individuals make informed decisions about their career paths, and aids in the development of skills necessary for professional growth. In this chapter, we will explore the definition, purpose, and role of career counseling in professional development, as well as current trends in the field.

Definition and Purpose of Career Counseling

Career counseling, also known as career guidance, is a process that helps individuals understand and appreciate their skills, interests, and values, and guides them in choosing a career path that aligns with these attributes. It is a collaborative process involving a counselor or coach and the individual seeking guidance.

The purpose of career counseling is multifaceted. It aims to help individuals:

Understand their career-related interests, abilities, and values.

Explore various career options and make informed decisions.

Develop job search skills, such as resume writing and interview techniques.

Navigate career transitions, such as job changes or retirement.

Address career-related challenges, such as job stress or dissatisfaction.

The Role of Career Counseling in Professional Development

Career counseling plays a pivotal role in professional development. It not only helps individuals make informed career decisions but also aids in the development of skills necessary for career advancement. Career counselors can provide resources and strategies for skill development, networking, and continuous learning, all of which are crucial for professional growth.

Moreover, career counseling can help individuals align their career goals with their personal growth goals, leading to increased job satisfaction and overall well-being. It can also assist individuals in navigating career transitions, managing work-life balance, and addressing job-related stress, contributing to a healthier professional life.

Current Trends in Career Counseling

Career counseling is continually evolving to meet the changing needs of the job market and workforce. Some current trends in the field include:

Holistic Approach: Career counseling is increasingly focusing on the whole person, considering factors like work-life balance, personal values, and overall well-being in career planning.

Technological Integration: Technology is playing a significant role in career counseling, with online counseling, career information systems, and digital career resources becoming more prevalent.

Lifelong Career Development: There is a growing recognition that career development is a lifelong process, and career counseling is expanding to address career issues across the lifespan.

Focus on Soft Skills: As the job market evolves, there is an increasing emphasis on soft skills, such as communication, problem-solving, and emotional intelligence, in career counseling.

In the following chapters, we will explore how Neuro-Linguistic Programming (NLP) can enhance these aspects of career counseling, providing valuable tools and strategies for career guidance and professional development.

Neuro-Linguistic Programming (NLP) has a significant role to play in the field of career counseling. Its principles and techniques can be applied to enhance the career counseling process, providing valuable tools for both counselors and clients. In this chapter, we will explore how NLP can be integrated into career counseling, illustrated with case studies, and discuss the benefits of using NLP in this context.

How NLP Principles Can Be Applied in Career Counseling

NLP principles can be effectively applied in career counseling in several ways:

Understanding and Changing Thought Patterns: NLP can help individuals identify and change limiting beliefs or thought patterns that may be hindering their career progress. For example, a person might believe they are not good enough for a particular job role. NLP techniques can help challenge and change this belief, enabling the person to explore new career opportunities.

Improving Communication: NLP techniques can enhance communication skills, which are crucial in job interviews and workplace interactions. Techniques such as mirroring and matching can help build rapport and create more effective communication.

Goal Setting and Achievement: NLP is excellent for setting and achieving career goals. Techniques such as the "Well-Formed Outcomes" can guide individuals in setting specific, achievable, and meaningful career goals.

Hypothetical Case Studies Showing the Application of NLP in Career Counseling

Case Study 1: A career counselor used NLP techniques to help a client overcome her fear of public speaking, which was hindering her career progression. Through techniques such as anchoring and visualization, the client was able to manage her anxiety and improve her public speaking skills, leading to a promotion at work.

Case Study 2: In another instance, a career counselor used NLP to assist a client in a career transition. The client was struggling with the decision to leave a secure job to start his own business. Using NLP reframing techniques, the counselor helped the client view the situation from different perspectives, enabling him to make a confident decision about his career move.

Benefits of Using NLP in Career Counseling

Using NLP in career counseling offers several benefits:

Enhanced Self-Awareness: NLP can help individuals gain a deeper understanding of their values, beliefs, and thought patterns, leading to increased self-awareness, a critical aspect of career development.

Improved Decision-Making: By changing limiting beliefs and enhancing communication with oneself, NLP can lead to improved decision-making, enabling individuals to make informed career choices.

Effective Goal Setting and Achievement: NLP provides practical tools for setting and achieving career goals, leading to more successful career outcomes.

In the next chapter, we will delve deeper into specific NLP techniques that can be used for professional development, providing practical strategies for career growth and advancement.

Chapter 4: NLP Techniques for Professional Development

Neuro-Linguistic Programming (NLP) offers a range of techniques that can be effectively applied for professional development. These techniques can help individuals enhance their communication skills, manage stress, set and achieve career goals, and more. In this chapter, we will explore some specific NLP techniques for professional development, discuss how to apply them in real-life situations, and share case studies and success stories.

Overview of Specific NLP Techniques for Professional Development

Anchoring: This technique involves associating a physical trigger or 'anchor' with a positive emotional state. For example, a professional might anchor the feeling of confidence to the action of tapping their fingers together. This anchor can then be used in situations such as job interviews or presentations to trigger the feeling of confidence.

Reframing: Reframing involves changing the way one perceives an event or situation to create a more positive or beneficial perspective. For instance, viewing a challenging project not as a problem, but as an opportunity for learning and growth.

Well-Formed Outcomes: This technique guides individuals in setting specific, achievable, and meaningful goals. It involves defining what one wants to achieve, identifying the resources needed, considering the impact of the goal on other areas of life, and setting a timeline for achievement.

Swish Pattern: This technique is used to change an unwanted behavior or response to a more desirable one. For example, replacing the habit of procrastination with the habit of taking immediate action.

How to Apply These Techniques in Real-Life Situations

Anchoring: Before a big presentation, use your anchor (e.g., tapping your fingers together) to trigger the feeling of confidence. Practice this regularly to strengthen the association.

Reframing: If you're feeling overwhelmed by a large project, reframe it as an opportunity to learn new skills and demonstrate your capabilities.

Well-Formed Outcomes: When setting career goals, ensure they are specific, measurable, achievable, relevant, and time-bound (SMART). Identify the resources you'll need, consider the impact on other areas of your life, and set a timeline for achievement.

Swish Pattern: If you find yourself procrastinating, visualize the action you're avoiding. Then, visualize yourself taking immediate action. 'Swish' the two images so that the image of procrastination is replaced by the image of taking action.

Hypothetical Case Studies and Success Stories

Case Study 1: A manager used the anchoring technique to boost her confidence during team meetings. She anchored the feeling of confidence to the action of holding her pen. Over time, she noticed a significant improvement in her ability to communicate her ideas effectively during meetings.

Case Study 2: A software developer used the well-formed outcomes technique to set a career goal of becoming a team lead. He defined his goal, identified the skills and experience he needed, considered the impact on his work-life balance, and set a timeline of two years. He achieved his goal within the set timeline, attributing his success to the structured approach of the well-formed outcomes technique.

These examples illustrate the practical application of NLP techniques in professional development. In the following chapters, we will explore the challenges and solutions in applying NLP in career counselling and look at the future trends of NLP in this field.

While Neuro-Linguistic Programming (NLP) offers valuable tools and techniques for career counseling, its application is not without challenges. In this chapter, we will explore some common challenges in applying NLP in career counseling and discuss practical solutions and strategies to overcome these challenges.

Common Challenges in Applying NLP in Career Counseling

Lack of Awareness and Understanding: Many individuals and even some career counselors are not aware of NLP or do not fully understand its principles and techniques. This lack of awareness and understanding can hinder the effective application of NLP in career counseling.

Skepticism About NLP: Some people are skeptical about NLP, questioning its scientific basis and effectiveness. This skepticism can create resistance to the use of NLP techniques in career counseling.

Training and Skill Requirements: Applying NLP techniques effectively requires training and skill. Not all career counselors have the necessary training to use NLP techniques, and even those who do may not always apply them effectively.

Individual Differences: NLP techniques may not work equally well for everyone. Individual differences in personality, learning style, and other factors can affect the effectiveness of NLP techniques.

Practical Solutions and Strategies to Overcome These Challenges

Promote Awareness and Understanding of NLP: Conduct workshops, seminars, and training programs to educate career counselors and clients about NLP. Provide resources such as books, articles, and online courses to enhance their understanding of NLP.

Address Skepticism with Evidence: Share research studies, case studies, and success stories that demonstrate the effectiveness of NLP in career counseling. Encourage skeptics to try NLP techniques for themselves before making a judgment.

Provide Training for Career Counselors: Offer training programs for career counselors to learn and practice NLP techniques. Provide ongoing support and supervision to ensure that they are applying the techniques effectively.

Tailor NLP Techniques to Individual Needs: Recognize that each individual is unique and may respond differently to NLP techniques. Tailor the techniques to the individual's needs, preferences, and learning style to enhance their effectiveness.

By addressing these challenges and implementing these solutions, we can enhance the application of NLP in career counseling, benefiting both career counselors and their clients. In the next chapter, we will explore the future trends of NLP in career counseling and professional development.

Neuro-Linguistic Programming (NLP) has already made
significant strides in the field of career counseling and
professional development. As we continue to understand more
about the human mind and behavior, the potential for NLP's
application in this field is vast. In this chapter, we will explore
the current research and advancements in NLP and discuss the
predicted trends for the future of NLP in career counseling and
professional development.

Current Research and Advancements in NLP

Integration with Technology: Recent advancements in NLP are
focused on integrating NLP techniques with technology. For
instance, NLP-based apps and online platforms are being
developed to provide self-help tools for personal and
professional development.

Enhanced Training Programs: Research is being conducted to
enhance NLP training programs, making them more effective
and accessible. This includes the development of online training
programs, which allow for wider access and flexibility.

Evidence-Based Practice: There is an increasing emphasis on
evidence-based practice in NLP. Researchers are conducting
studies to evaluate the effectiveness of NLP techniques and to
identify factors that may influence their effectiveness.

Predicted Trends for the Future of NLP in Career Counseling and Professional Development

Increased Use of Technology: The use of technology in applying NLP techniques is expected to increase. This includes the use of AI and machine learning to personalize NLP-based interventions and the use of virtual reality to enhance the practice of NLP techniques.

Greater Integration with Other Approaches: NLP is likely to be integrated more with other approaches in career counseling and professional development. This includes approaches such as cognitive-behavioral therapy, mindfulness, and positive psychology.

Wider Acceptance and Use: As more research supports the effectiveness of NLP, its acceptance and use in career counseling and professional development are likely to increase. This includes its use in various settings, such as schools, colleges, organizations, and career counseling centers.

In conclusion, the future of NLP in career counseling and professional development looks promising. As we continue to explore and understand the potential of NLP, it can serve as a powerful tool to help individuals achieve their career goals and realize their professional potential.

Conclusion

This book has taken a comprehensive look at the role of Neuro-Linguistic Programming (NLP) in career counseling and professional development. We began with an introduction to the field, exploring the importance of career counseling and the basics of NLP. We then delved into the specifics of NLP, understanding its principles and techniques, and how they can be applied to personal and professional development.

In the subsequent chapters, we examined the importance of career counseling and how NLP can be integrated into this process. We discussed specific NLP techniques for professional development and provided real-life examples and case studies to illustrate their application. We also addressed the challenges in applying NLP in career counseling and offered practical solutions to overcome these challenges.

In the final chapters, we looked at the future of NLP in career counseling and professional development, discussing current research, advancements, and predicted trends. We explored how technology is being integrated with NLP and how NLP is likely to be combined with other approaches in the future.

In conclusion, NLP offers a powerful set of tools and techniques that can significantly enhance career counseling and professional development. While there are challenges in applying NLP, with the right training and approach, these can be overcome. The future of NLP in this field looks promising, with advancements in technology and research likely to further enhance its application.

The role of NLP in career counseling and professional development is a vast and evolving field. As we continue to explore and understand this potential, NLP can serve as a powerful tool to help individuals achieve their career goals and realize their professional potential. It is our hope that this book has provided valuable insights into this exciting field and will serve as a useful guide for career counselors, professionals, and anyone interested in personal and professional development.

About the Author

Rex Morton is a renowned author and researcher in the United Kingdom with a passionate interest in the human mind, specifically in Cognitive Behavioural Therapy (CBT) and Neuro-Linguistic Programming (NLP).

Morton has spent a considerable portion of his professional life diving deep into the theories and principles that form the backbone of these two compelling fields. His fascination with NLP led him to complete an extensive certification program, solidifying his understanding of this innovative approach to understanding human behaviour.

Although Morton does not have clinical experience, his intense curiosity and dedication to studying these subjects have made him a respected figure in the field. He has thoroughly researched the integration of NLP techniques into CBT, offering fresh perspectives and insights into how these two methodologies can complement each other to enhance understanding of human cognition and behaviour.

As an author, Morton has successfully communicated his knowledge and passion to a broader audience, making complex psychological theories accessible to professionals and interested laypersons. His writing is characterized by a clear, engaging style and a focus on the practical application of theories, making them relevant to everyday life.

In his personal life, Morton is an ardent lover of the natural world, often spending his free time exploring the British countryside. His passion for landscape photography allows him to capture and share the beauty of these excursions. Despite his accomplishments, Morton is known for his humility and eagerness to continue learning. His work continues to inspire those interested in the intricate workings of the human mind and the exciting possibilities presented by the integration of NLP and CBT.

If you've found the content of this book enlightening and wish to continue your journey of understanding the human mind, I warmly invite you to visit my website at www.rexmorton.com. The website serves as a hub of knowledge where I share my latest findings, thoughts, and insights on the integration of NLP and CBT.

I also encourage you to subscribe to the newsletter available on the website. By subscribing, you'll receive regular updates on a range of topics, from detailed discussions on specific NLP techniques and their application in CBT, to the latest research in the field.

The newsletter is also the first place I'll share news of upcoming releases. Whether it's the announcement of a new book, the launch of an online course, newsletter subscribers will be the first to know. This is a great opportunity to continue learning directly from me, deepening your understanding of NLP and CBT, and enhancing your skills in applying these techniques in your own life or professional practice.

I'm looking forward to sharing this journey with you.

www.ingramcontent.com/pod-product-compliance
Lightning Source LLC
Chambersburg PA
CBHW072229290526
45794CB00007B/2944